FUNNY BONES

Posada and His Day of the Dead *Calaveras*

DUNCAN TONATIUH

Abrams Books for Young Readers ❋ **New York**

Skeletons riding bicycles . . . skeletons swearing fancy hats . . . skeletons dancing and strumming on guitars. We call these festive bony figures *calaveras*. In Spanish, the word *calavera* [ca-la-VEH-rah] means "skull." A lot of things that are associated with skulls and with *el Día de Muertos*—the Day of the Dead—are called calaveras. For example, there are calavera drawings, candy calaveras, calavera poems, and calavera toys. The skeleton figures are not scary—in fact, they look as if they're having fun.

They are the creation of José Guadalupe Posada, and this is his story.

In 1852, in a small house in the Mexican city of Aguascalientes,
José Guadalupe Posada was born. Lupe [LOO-peh], as everyone called him,
was the son of a baker and the sixth of eight children.

Lupe's older brother Cirilo became a teacher. He taught Lupe how to read and write. Lupe loved to copy the drawings he saw in prints and in books at school. Cirilo noticed how well Lupe drew and helped him enroll at the local art academy.

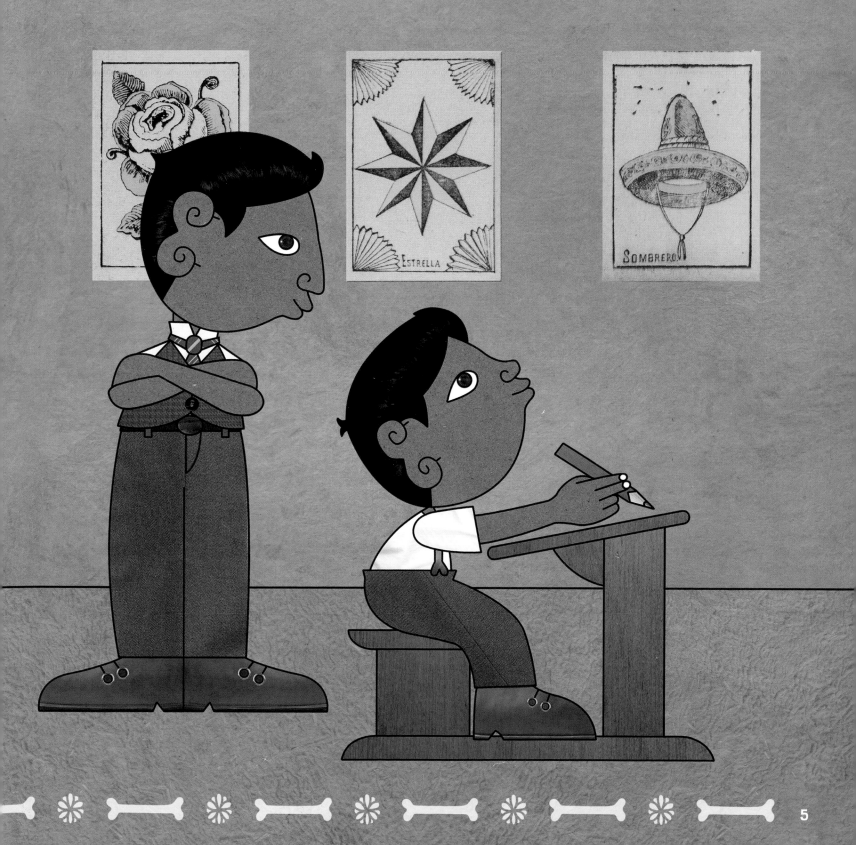

When Lupe was eighteen years old, he began to work at Don Trinidad Pedroza's print shop. There he discovered his lifelong passion for printing. He learned lithography.

1. Using a grease pencil, draw on a special flat limestone.

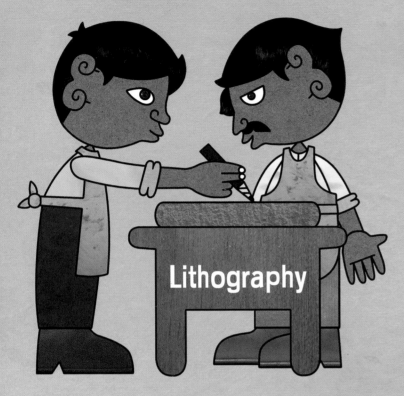

2. Apply chemicals and moisten the stone with water.

3. Cover the stone with an oil-based ink. The ink will adhere only to the drawing, because water and oil don't mix.

4. Use a press to print the image on a piece of paper. Repeat as many times as you wish.

Lupe also learned engraving. He helped Don Trinidad print documents, diplomas, flyers, labels for matchbooks, receipts, and invitations for weddings and birthdays.

1. Draw on a piece of wood or a metal plate.

Engraving

2. Use a cutting tool called a "burin" to carve around the drawing. This will cause the drawing to be raised above the rest of the plate.

4. Use a press to print the image on a piece of paper. Repeat as many times as you wish.

3. Cover the drawing with ink. The ink will adhere only to the parts that are "in relief"—that is, raised.

After work, Lupe, Don Trinidad, and other artisans would gather at the shop. They were unhappy with the job that the people in the government were doing. Don Trinidad invited Lupe to make some drawings for a small newspaper he was involved with. It was called *el Jicote*, "The Bumblebee." Lupe drew cartoons for the paper. This was long before he drew calaveras. In one of his drawings, Lupe drew some local politicians climbing a pole and stepping over one another. By making the men look silly, he showed their greed and other bad traits.

Readers of *el Jicote* agreed with Lupe's point of view and laughed when they saw his cartoons. That year, some of the politicians Lupe and Don Trinidad were against lost the elections. But some remained in power and were angry at them. To avoid trouble, Lupe and Don Trinidad decided to move to the nearby city of León.

Lupe lived in León for many years. He opened his own print shop, and everyone began to call him *Don* Lupe as a sign of respect. He married María de Jesús Vela, and eventually they had a son. They named him Juan Sabino. In addition to his printing work, Don Lupe began to create illustrations for books and pamphlets. He also taught lithography at a local school. He became successful and well known in the region.

But in 1888 a terrible flood destroyed a large part of the city, including Don Lupe's shop.

Don Lupe, his wife, and their son moved to Mexico City, the capital of the country. Don Lupe worked as an illustrator and a designer in several print shops. Eventually, he was able to open his own shop near the Zócalo, the city's main square.

One of the men Don Lupe worked with was Antonio Vanegas. He published intriguing stories on large sheets of bright paper called "broadsides." The tales were about a wide range of topics, including scary creatures, fires, miracles, violent crimes, heroes, bandits, cockfights, and bullfighters. Don Lupe illustrated many of these tales. Paperboys sold the inexpensive broadsides on the streets for a few cents, and people—even people who couldn't read—bought them. They were fascinated by Don Lupe's drawings!

Don Lupe and Don Antonio worked together for more than twenty years. They were always busy, especially every November 1–2, during the Día de Muertos celebrations.

On those days, the city was full of vendors who sold *pan de muerto* (bread), *cempasúchil* (marigold flowers), *alfeñiques* (sugar skulls), and *papel picado* (paper cutouts). People bought these and other items to decorate the *ofrendas* (offerings) they made for their loved ones who had died.

For the holiday, Don Antonio and other editors published literary calaveras. They were short rhyming poems that featured a skeleton and made jokes about him or her. People found the poems very funny and bought them on the street from paperboys. A man named Manuel Manilla illustrated many of these poems for Don Antonio. Don Lupe also began to illustrate them, and soon he became a master at it.

La calaca tapatia
estaba paseando un dia
cuando se sintio mal
y se tomo un mezcal

La calavera carpintera
con serrucho y con tijera
tenia un bonito sombrero
que le vendió el bodeguero

CALAVERA LOVE

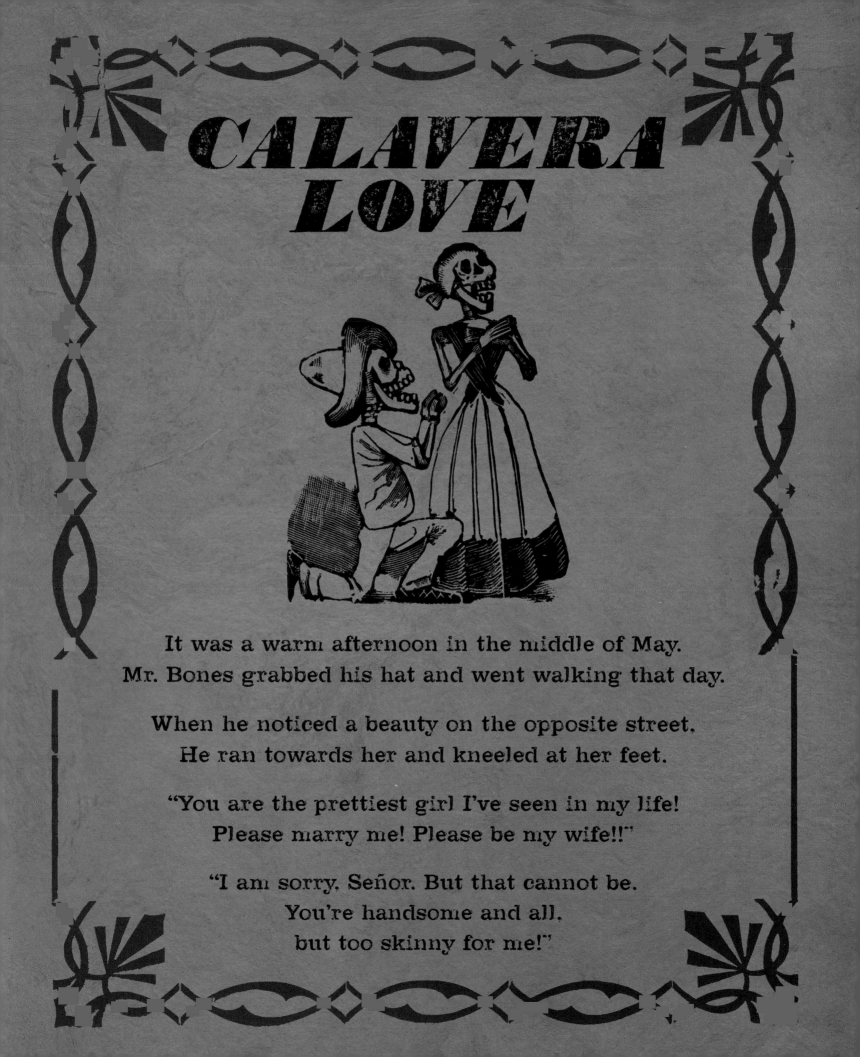

It was a warm afternoon in the middle of May.
Mr. Bones grabbed his hat and went walking that day.

When he noticed a beauty on the opposite street,
He ran towards her and kneeled at her feet.

"You are the prettiest girl I've seen in my life!
Please marry me! Please be my wife!!"

"I am sorry, Señor. But that cannot be.
You're handsome and all,
but too skinny for me!"

Don Lupe had a lot of work. He was busy all the time! He began using a printing technique that was quicker than lithography or engraving. It was called "etching."

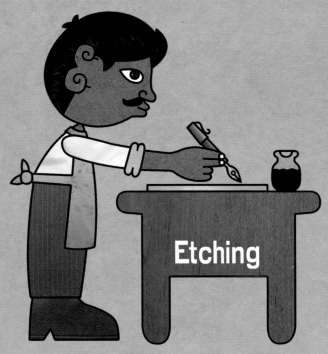

1. Using a pen and acid-resistant ink, draw on a metal plate.

2. Dip the plate in acid. The acid will make the top layer disintegrate, leaving just the drawing.

3. Cover the plate with ink. The ink will adhere only to the parts that are in relief (raised).

4. Use a press to print the image on a piece of paper.

Don Lupe made thousands of drawings over the years. Only a hundred or so are of calaveras, but they are now his most famous images. Whether he made an etching, a lithograph, or an engraving, he had to draw the image in reverse—the opposite of the way he wanted the finished image to appear. Otherwise, when the image was transferred by ink to paper, it would be backwards!

The inspiration behind some of Don Lupe's calaveras is clear, but for others it is not. We can try to interpret what they mean.

During el Día de Muertos, Don Lupe surely watched people going to the cemetery. They weeded and repainted the gravestones of their loved ones. They brought food and told stories about them. Sometimes they hired musicians to play their loved ones' favorite songs.

DON LUPE DREW SOME SKELETONS
DANCING AND PARTYING.
WAS HE SAYING THAT...

...EL DIA DE MUERTOS IS NOT
ONLY A CELEBRATION OF DEATH
BUT ALSO A CELEBRATION OF LIFE?
A DAY WHEN THE DEAD
BECOME ALIVE?

One day, Don Lupe drew a skeleton wearing a flamboyant hat: la Catrina. The drawing was printed alongside a calavera poem about the type of woman who puts on makeup and fancy clothes and acts as if she's better than everyone else. Can you imagine the woman who inspired that drawing? Perhaps she wore a pretentious outfit and strolled through the park on a Sunday afternoon. She thought highly of herself, but acted mean and ignored others when they needed help.

Was Don Lupe saying that ...

... no matter how fancy your clothes are on the outside, on the inside we are all the same? That we are all calaveras?

Don Lupe saw his country—and especially Mexico City—change dramatically during his lifetime. When he was a boy, people walked or rode on horses or in carriages. Now he saw people riding on bicycles. He saw streetcars travel on tracks through the city. Everyone seemed to be going faster and faster.

DON LUPE DREW SOME WILD
SKELETONS RACING AND
TRAMPLING ONE ANOTHER.
WAS HE SAYING THAT...

...WE CAN TRY TO GO FASTER
BUT ONE DAY WE WILL ALL
REACH THE SAME FINISH LINE
AND BECOME CALAVERAS?

In 1910, when Don Lupe was fifty-eight years old, a terrible conflict began. Today it is referred to as the "Mexican Revolution." Thousands of farmers and workers throughout Mexico were angry because they worked very hard but could barely earn enough money for their families to live on.

The laborers grabbed rifles, machetes, sticks, and any weapons they could find to fight the government and the wealthy landlords it protected. But the rebellious groups that formed in different parts of the country did not work together. They began to fight not only the government but one another as well, and things spun out of control. Thousands of people lost their lives.

Most of Don Lupe's calaveras are festive and fun.

But the ones he drew about *la Revolución* are aggressive and frightening. Was Don Lupe saying that sometimes calaveras are not a laughing matter?

Don Lupe drew some of the leaders who were involved in la Revolución, like Emiliano Zapata and Francisco I. Madero. His calaveras were a way to criticize those men and express his own views.

EMILIANO ZAPATA   FRANCISCO I. MADERO

He would praise them if he agreed with their decisions and actions. But he would ridicule them if he disagreed with them, just as he had poked fun at the politicians in Aguascalientes when he was a young man.

WAS DON LUPE SAYING THAT...

EMILIANO ZAPATA

FRANCISCO I. MADERO

...EVEN POWERFUL LEADERS ONE DAY BECOME CALAVERAS?

*Esta si es la calavera
del editor popular
divertida la mera mera
como musica pá bailar*

Don Lupe drew calaveras of famous men, but he also drew calaveras of the people around him, like the men who swept the streets and the people who worked at print shops. He even drew a calavera of his friend Don Antonio.

WAS DON LUPE SAYING THAT . . .

. . . CALAVERAS ARE ALL AROUND US? THAT WE ARE ALL CALAVERAS, WHETHER WE ARE RICH OR POOR, FAMOUS OR NOT?

Don Lupe died on January 20, 1913. Many people were familiar with his drawings and his calaveras, but very few people knew the artist who was behind them. It was years after his death that historians and artists such as Jean Charlot and Diego Rivera began to wonder who had drawn such wonderful images.

Today, José Guadalupe Posada is not called Don Lupe anymore. He is simply called Posada, which is the way he signed his work. His art is celebrated in Mexico, in the United States, and around the world. Some people even dress like Catrinas and parade on the streets during el Día de Muertos. And on that special day there is always somewhere an altar with an ofrenda to remember the great Don Lupe Posada.

AUTHOR'S NOTE

El Día de Muertos, or the Day of the Dead, is a festive and often humorous holiday in which people remember their deceased loved ones. It is celebrated every November 1–2 throughout Mexico and in many parts of the United States and Central America. Similar holidays exist in other parts of the world. November 1 is dedicated to children, and November 2 is dedicated to adults who have died. In 2003, the United Nations Educational, Scientific and Cultural Organization (UNESCO) named el Día de Muertos an intangible cultural heritage of humanity.

The holiday has its origin in Pre-Columbian times. Many cultures in the Americas held festivities to celebrate the dead. The Aztecs, for instance, had a month-long celebration every year to honor Mictlantecuhtli and Mictecacíhuatl, the god and goddess of death. For these ancient cultures, death was not seen as the end of living but, instead, as another step in the cycle of life.

When the Spanish conquered the Aztecs and other peoples of the Americas, much of the natives' way of life was lost. But some of their traditions and beliefs survived and mixed with the beliefs and customs of the European conquerors. Such is the case with el Día de Muertos, which is celebrated on the Catholic holiday of All Hallows, or All Saints' Day.

El Día de Muertos is celebrated different ways, varying from region to region. People often go to the cemetery to pray. They weed and repaint the gravestones of their loved ones. They bring their loved ones' favorite food and tell stories about them. Sometimes they hire musicians to play their loved ones' favorite songs. They have a picnic and spend the whole day at the cemetery. In some places they spend the entire night there too.

At home, people build an altar with an *ofrenda*, or offering. They often include a picture of any relatives and friends who have passed away. Many people believe that during el Día de Muertos the spirit of the deceased travels back from the afterlife to again be with his or her family and friends. Day of the Dead ofrendas are made not only at home; they are also made at schools, libraries, museums, and in other public places. Sometimes they are dedicated to an artist or hero who is no longer alive. The Posada museum in Aguascalientes has an ofrenda for José Guadalupe Posada every year.

There are different crafts and decorations that people typically use to decorate ofrendas and gravestones. *Cempasúchil* flowers, bright orange marigolds, are sold at markets and outside cemeteries during el Día de Muertos. Bakers often bake *pan de muerto*, a round bread decorated with bonelike shapes. Vendors sell *alfeñiques*, figurines made out of sugar, and *papel picado*, among other crafts and toys. Crosses, candles, and other religious iconography are usually included in ofrendas too.

Literary *calaveras*, or calavera poems, are another important expression of el Día de Muertos. Literary calaveras are short humorous poems that rhyme and that involve death

in some kind of way. The poems often imagine how a person encounters death or how the person becomes a calavera. Calavera poems are written every year, especially about powerful and famous people, like presidents, politicians, artists, and athletes.

The poems became popular in the late 1800s. After Mexico won its independence from Spain in 1810, the country gained more freedom of the press and a lot of newspapers and publications began to appear. Calavera poems became an acceptable way to poke fun at elected and appointed officials.

José Guadalupe Posada was not the first to illustrate calavera poems, but he was certainly the most prolific and the best at it. The editor Antonio Vanegas had worked with an illustrator named Manuel Manilla for several years before he began working with Posada. Some calavera drawings that are often attributed to Posada are now known to have been drawn by Manilla. Very little is known of Manilla and of his life. Even less is known about artists who drew calaveras before Manilla and Posada.

Posada made calavera drawings every Día de Muertos for twenty-four years. Although his drawings and calveras were popular while he was alive, Posada died a poor man. Very few people knew he was the artist behind such great drawings.

It was years after Posada's death that Jean Charlot, a French-born American painter, discovered his images while in Mexico and began to collect his work. Charlot tried to learn more about Posada. In 1925, he wrote an essay about him; in 1930, he co-edited a catalog of

his work. These publications revived interest in Posada's work and made Posada's name and work known to other artists and to the public at large.

Famous Mexican muralists like Diego Rivera and Jose Clemente Orozco were greatly influenced by Posada, and they celebrated his work. Nowadays, museums, galleries, and universities in Mexico, the United States, and other parts of the world have collections of Posada's work, including the actual printing plates from which his prints were made. Many books have been written about Posada, but facts about his life are still being discovered.

In an essay, Diego Rivera wrote that Posada's name may one day be forgotten but his work will always be a part of Mexico's popular arts. In many ways, this is true today. Reproductions of Posada's artwork are typically used during el Dia de Muertos. They have become part of the celebration's imagery. His calaveras are much more famous than his name. They capture the festive sentiment of el Dia de Muertos holiday.

Although they were made during a specific time period, Posada's calaveras have a universal and timeless quality. They make us ask questions about life and death. This book is a tribute to the great Don Lupe Posada, and I hope it offers an opportunity to ponder the meaning behind his calaveras. It is also an opportunity to learn and celebrate el Dia de Muertos, a wonderful holiday that is not only a celebration of death but also a celebration of life.

GLOSSARY

alfeñique [al-fen-YEE-keh]: Sugar figurine. During el Día de Muertos, vendors sell alfeñiques and people buy them to decorate their ofrendas. The figurines are usually of calaveras. The skulls are sometimes made out of chocolate, and they are often decorated with a name. People buy calaveras inscribed with the names of their deceased loved ones. The figurines can also be of animals or food.

broadsides: A type of inexpensive publication that was very common between the sixteenth and nineteenth centuries. Broadsides were large pieces of paper. The text of the story was printed on only one side of the page, and there was usually a large illustration to go with it.

calavera [ca-la-VEH-rah]: Calavera means "skull" in Spanish. Calaveras are not meant to be scary but, rather, festive and fun.

cartoons: Cartoons are drawings that are meant to poke fun at someone or something. If the cartoon is of a person, his or her features—like nose or ears—are often exaggerated. Political cartoons are used to criticize politicians and other people in power.

la Catrina: The female dandy or the dapper. When la Catrina was first published, it was called la Calavera Garbancera. "Garbancera" was a name given to women who powdered their faces to hide their brown skin and look white. Diego Rivera is the one that coined the term la Catrina. After Rivera called the drawing la Catrina, everyone began calling it that. It has become the drawing's popular name.

cempasúchil [sem-pa-SOO-cheel]: A bright orange marigold.

Jean Charlot [shar-LOW]: A French-born American painter who spent a significant portion of his life in Mexico. He is generally recognized as the person who "discovered" Posada. When Posada was alive, his work was popular, but few people knew who the actual artist was. When Charlot saw Posada's images for the first time in 1922, he was immediately struck by them and began collecting them. He searched for Posada's printing plates and tried to learn more about his life. In 1925, he wrote an essay about him; in 1930, he co-edited a catalog of Posada's work. These publications helped Posada's name and work become known to other artists and the public at large.

el Día de Muertos [el DEE-ah day MWEAR-tohs] (the Day of the Dead): A holiday in which people remember loved ones who have passed away. It is celebrated every November 1–2 throughout Mexico and in many parts of the United States and Central America.

don: Spanish for "Mister." It's a respectful way to address male adults and is similar to "Señor."

engraving: A printmaking technique that can be traced to Mesopotamia 3000 years ago. There are different types of engraving. The engraving technique that Posada practiced was a relief printing technique. In it, the artist makes a drawing on a surface, usually a wood or metal plate. He then uses tools, such as a burin, to carve around the drawing. The plate is then covered with ink. The ink will cover only the section that is in relief or is raised or embossed. A press is then used to print the image on paper.

etching: A printmaking technique that dates back to the 1500s. In etching, acid is used to bite or disintegrate the areas of a metal plate that are not covered by an acid-resistant substance. The etching technique that Posada practiced was different from traditional etching techniques. He printed the section of the plate that was in relief or raised. Traditionally, prints of etchings are prints of the section of the plate that is sunk or "intaglio."

lithography [lih-THOG-ruh-fee]: A printmaking technique that was invented in 1796. It is based on the principle that oil and water don't mix. The artist draws with a grease pencil on a special flat limestone. After treating the stone with gum arabic and other chemicals, the stone is moistened with water. The stone is then covered with an oil-based ink. The ink will adhere only to the grease pencil drawing and not to the moist areas. A press is then used to print the drawing on paper, one time or multiple times. Many things like posters and books continue to be printed today by a modern offset lithographic process.

Mexican Revolution (la Revolución) [la re-voh-loo-see-ON]: An armed conflict that began in 1910 and lasted approximately ten years. The conflict began when Francisco I. Madero decided to take up arms against Porfirio Diaz, a dictator who had ruled Mexico for almost thirty years. After Madero's uprising, different armies led by people like Emiliano Zapata, Pancho Villa, and Venustiano Carranza formed in different parts of the country. The leaders had different interests, however, and their armies began to fight one another. La Revolución was an extremely violent conflict, and some historians estimate that more then a million people lost their lives during it. One of the outcomes of la Revolución was the Mexican Constitution of 1917, which is Mexico's current governing document.

ofrenda [off-REN-dah]: Offering.

pan de muerto [pahn de MWEAR-toh]: A type of bread that is made specially for el Día de Muertos. The bread is round and is decorated with bonelike shapes. Families often include pan de muerto in their ofrendas.

papel picado [pah-PEL pee-CAH-doh]: Paper cutouts. They are bright, decorative sheets of paper that are perforated to create designs. Day of the Dead papel picado often include images of calaveras.

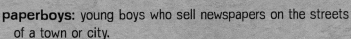

paperboys: young boys who sell newspapers on the streets of a town or city.

Diego Rivera: Perhaps the most famous Mexican painter and muralist. He was greatly influenced by Posada's work. He wrote an essay about Posada that was included in the 1930 catalog that Jean Charlot co-edited. He included portraits of Posada in some of his murals, like the mural called *Dream of a Sunday Afternoon in Alameda Park* (1948). In the mural, Rivera painted himself as a boy. He shows himself holding la Calavera Catrina's hand. Posada is on the opposite side of la Catrina, holding her arm.

BIBLIOGRAPHY

José Guadalupe Posada

Barajas Durán, Rafael. *Posada: Mito y mitote: La caricatura política de José Guadalupe Posada y Manuel Alfonso Manila.* México City: Fondo de Cultura Economica, 2009.

Berdecio, Roberto, and Stanley Appelbaum, eds. *Posada's Popular Mexican Prints: 273 Cuts by José Guadalupe Posada.* New York: Dover Publications, 1972.

Bonilla Reyna, Helia Emma, ed. *José Guadalupe Posada: A 100 años de su partida.* México City: Instituto Cultural de Aguascalientes, Banamex, 2012.

Carrillo Azpeitia, Rafael. *Posada y el grabado mexicano: Desde el famoso grabador de temas populares hasta los artistas contemporáneos.* México City: Panorama Editorial, 1991.

Frank, Patrick. *Posada's Broadsheets: Mexican Popular Imagery, 1890–1910.* Albuquerque: University of New Mexico Press, 1998.

José Guadalupe Posada: Edición conmemorativa. Aguascalientes, México: Instituto Cultural de Aguascalientes; México City: Consejo Nacional para la Cultura y las Artes, 2013.

López Casillas, Mercurio. *Images of Death in Mexican Prints.* México City: Editorial RM, 2008.

——. *José Guadalupe Posada: Illustrator of Chapbooks.* México City: Editorial RM, 2005.

——. *Posada: El grabador mexicano.* Seville, Spain: Centro Andaluz de Arte Contemporáneo; México City: Editorial RM, 2005.

Rothenstein, Julian, ed. *J. G. Posada: Messenger of Mortality.* Mount Kisco, N.Y.: Moyer Bell, 1989.

Toor, Frances, Paul O'Higgins, and Blas Vanegas Arroyo, eds. *Monografía: Las obras de José Guadalupe Posada.* México City: Mexican Folkways, 1930.

Topete del Valle, Alejandro. *José Guadalupe Posada: Notorious Promoter of Popular Mexican Graphic Art.* Aguascalientes, México: Universidad Autonoma de Aguascalientes, 2007.

Tyler, Ron, ed. *Posada's Mexico.* Washington, D.C.: Library of Congress, 1979.

Manuel Manilla

Bonilla Reyna, Helia Emma. *Manuel Manilla: Protagonista de los cambios en el grabado decimonónico.* México City: Circulo de Arte, 2000.

López Casillas, Mercurio. *Monograph of 598 Prints by Mexican Engraver Manuel Manilla.* México City: Editorial RM, 2005.

Martínez, Jesús. *Historia del grabado.* 2 vols. Guanajuato, México: Ediciones La Rana, 2006.

Printmaking

Heller, Jules. *Printmaking Today: A Studio Handbook.* New York: Holt, Rinehart and Winston, 1972.

Saff, Donald, and Deli Sacilotto. *Printmaking: History and Process.* New York: Holt, Rinehart and Winston, 1978.

ART CREDITS

ART CREDITS FOR WORK NOT BY DUNCAN TONATIUH
Exact date of execution unknown, but circa late 19th and early 20th centuries. Posada artworks on pages 2, 3, and 5 are colored by the author. Posada's black-and-white prints, especially the book covers he illustrated, were often colored in a similar fashion.

José Guadalupe Posada: Cover: Details of images found in the text; Pages 2–3: Details of later images, except for the calavera with guitar titled "El gran panteón amoroso" (The Big Cemetery of Lovers). Broadside. Colored by Duncan Tonatiuh. Page 5: Details from "El Juego de Lotería" (The Lottery Game). Board game. Colored by Duncan Tonatiuh. Page 9: *El Jicote* 5 (1871). Page 13: Detail of "Al C. General Porfirio Díaz" (To C. General Porfirio Diaz). Broadside. Page 17: Illustration from "La calavera de Cupido" (Calavera of Cupid). Broadside. Page 19: "Calavera Don Juan Tenorio" (Calavera of Don Juan Tenorio) *Left:* simulation of zinc plate. *Right:* Broadside. Page 21: "Gran fandango y francachela de todas las calaveras" (Happy Dance and Wild Party of all the Skeletons). Broadside. Page 23: "Calavera Garbancera" (Calavera of the Fashionable Lady). Broadside. Years after Posada's death, Diego Rivera coined the name "Calavera Catrina," which is how the artwork is primarily known. Page 25: "Calavera las bicicletas" (Calavera of the Cyclists). Broadside. Page 27: "La calavera oaxoqueña" (The Oaxaca Calavera); Broadside. Page 29: *Left:* "La calavera de Emiliano Zapata" (Calavera of Emiliano Zapata). Broadside. *Right:* "Calavera de Madero" (Calavera of Madero). Broadside. Page 30: "Calavera del Catrín" (Calavera of the Dandy). Broadside. Page 31: "Calavera de los patinadores" (Calavera of the Street Cleaners). Broadside.
Manuel Manilla Page 16: *Top:* "Calavera Tapatía" (Calavera from Guadalajara). *Bottom:* "Calavera de la gente" (The People's Calavera). Broadsides.

WHERE YOU CAN SEE POSADA'S WORK IN THE U.S.A.

Amon Carter Museum of American Art, Fort Worth, Texas;
cartermuseum.org
Art Institute of Chicago; artic.edu
Bancroft Library, University of California, Berkeley;
bancroft.berkeley.edu
Jean Charlot Collection, Thomas Hale Hamilton Library,
University of Hawaii at Manoa, Honolulu;
libweb.hawaii.edu/libdept/charlotcoll/charlot.html
Colorado Springs Fine Arts Center, Colorado; csfineartscenter.org
Library of Congress, Washington, DC; loc.gov
Metropolitan Museum of Art, New York; metmuseum.org
Museum of Modern Art, New York; moma.org
New York Public Library; nypl.org
Harry Ransom Center, University of Texas at Austin; hrc.utexas.edu
Arizona State University Art Museum, Tempe; asuartm.edu

INDEX

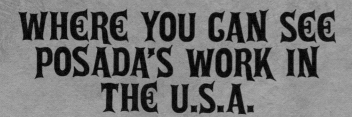

TO MY ABUELITOS, ABUELITAS, AND ANCESTORS

The artwork in this book was hand-drawn, then collaged digitally. The book also features art by José Guadalupe Posada and Manuel Manilla, sometimes within Duncan Tonatiuh's illustrations and sometimes standing alone. Please see the art credits for titles.

Library of Congress Cataloging-in-Publication Data

Tonatiuh, Duncan.
Funny bones : Posada and his Day of the Dead calaveras / by Duncan Tonatiuh.
pages cm
ISBN 978-1-4197-1647-8
1. Posada, José Guadalupe, 1852–1913—Biography—Juvenile literature. 2. Engravers—Mexico—Biography—Juvenile literature. 3. Human skeleton in art—Juvenile literature. I. Title.
NE546.P6T65 2015
769.92—dc23
2014042319

Text and illustrations copyright © 2015 Duncan Tonatiuh
Book design by Maria T. Middleton

Printed and bound in China
10 9 8 7 6 5 4 3 2 1

Abrams Books for Young Readers are available at special discounts when purchased in quantity for premiums and promotions as well as fundraising or educational use. Special editions can also be created to specification. For details, contact specialsales@abramsbooks.com or the address below.

ABRAMS
THE ART OF BOOKS SINCE 1949
115 West 18th Street
New York, NY 10011
www.abramsbooks.com